The Lloy
1
L
Te

Loved By Two

This is a book about a blended family due to same sex parenting. It is this author's hope that this book will open up conversations about diversity. Children need to know they are loved and they need to understand differences. My hope is that, we as parents are sensitive to the challenges our children face. Sometimes their challenges are due to our choices and we need to embrace what they feel enough to teach them that love has no bounds. They are LOVED!

Sarah stood by her window and watched the rain dance across the window.

"Sweetheart, time for your bedtime snack." Mom's voice echoed up the stairs.

"Be right down."

Sarah ran downstairs, and took a big bite of her banana waiting for her.

"Hmm. Good." After finishing her banana, she looked at the floor. "Mommy." Sarah kicked her feet and made doodles with her finger on the table.

"You know," she said, "I have to write about how families are alike and how they are different for a class project this week."

Mom wiped the kitchen table and threw the banana peel in the trash.

"Oh, that's interesting, Sweetie."

"Yeah, I guess. But, do you know that no one in my class has two mommies? I feel weird and different."

"Really?" said Mom. She turned toward the doorway and yelled, "Linda."

Linda came to the doorway. "Yes."

"I think it's time we have a talk with Sarah." Mom took Sarah's hand and Linda's hand and led them into the living room.

"Honey, sit down," said Linda. Sarah sat on the couch and Mom sat next to her.

"You're right, Sweetheart," said Mom, "our family does look different. But, that's okay. Everyone is different in one way or another. Be proud of who you are no matter what." Mom gave Sarah a big hug. "Come on, I'll tuck you into bed."

Sarah scrambled into bed and brought the blanket up to her chin.

Mom tucked it snug around her and gave her a kiss. "Good night. Sleep well. I love you."

"Good night Mom. I love you too." Mom turned the light off and went downstairs.

Linda sat at the kitchen table waiting to discuss their problem.

Mom walked into the kitchen after tucking Sarah into bed and said, "I don't know how I feel about this week's class project, Linda. I may need to speak with Sarah's teacher tomorrow."

"Oh, don't be silly, Janice. It's a fun and harmless little project. What would be the point?

Janice sat down and grabbed a cookie from the cookie jar.

"The point is that it's making my little girl feel different than her friends. It makes her stand out from the rest of her class. How does she explain that you're my special friend and that we're a family?"

Linda nodded. "Okay, I see your point. Let's sleep on it and see how you feel in the morning."

Sarah woke early. She washed her face and brushed her teeth then went downstairs for breakfast. "Mom, have you seen my back pack?

"It's by the door, Sweetie."

Sarah gobbled down her food and grabbed her back pack. She hugged and kissed Linda and Mom then went to the school bus stop.

The day went quick. After school, Sarah raced to the bus and jumped on. She looked around then sat next to her friends. "Hey Jack, have you done the class project with your parents yet?"

Jack shook his head. "No, I don't want to do the stupid project."

"Why not?" asked Sarah.

"I have two dads in my house and Billy and Ryan always make fun of me because of that. I don't want to tell the whole class about it. They'll all make fun of me too."

"Do you want to know a secret, Jack? I have two mommies in my house. My Mom told me that it's okay to look different and we should not be embarrassed or ashamed because other people's families don't look like ours. We have to be proud of ourselves no matter what."

"You're right, Sarah. But, doesn't it embarrass you to have two mommies?"

Sarah nodded. "Yeah, sometimes, but my Mom told me that you can't control who you love. The most important thing to remember is that our parents love us."

Jack jumped up. "This is my stop." I'll see you tomorrow.

"Okay. Bye Jack, see you tomorrow."

The next stop was Sarah's. She got off the bus, ran home, dashed inside and threw her backpack on the floor. "Hi Mom. Hi Linda.

Can I go in the backyard to play?"

"Sure." Said Linda.

Sarah played on her swing set until dinner time. After dinner, she pulled out her homework. "Mom will you help me with my project now?"

"Sure Sweetie."

Sarah thought of the first way that their family was different:

1. I have two mommies.

2.

Mom said. "Hey, number two should be that there are families who love differently. Put that down."

"Loves differently?" asked Sarah.

"Yes," said Linda. There are all different kinds of love and families. No one loves exactly the same."

Mom put her arm over Sarah's shoulders. "That's right. Our family is a family that loves. We love you so much, Sweetheart."

Sarah shrugged her shoulders. "I don't feel loved when my friends at school make fun of me because I have two mommies."

"Oh, Sweetie," said Mom. "I'm so sorry. I didn't know they made fun of you."

"Yeah, my friends say that there is no such thing as two mommies, only a mommy and a daddy. Why can't my daddy come back home?

Even my friend Jack was sad because he lives with his dad and his dad's special friend. The other kids at school say he is going to be a queer just like his daddy. My other friend is adopted and people make fun of her too. They call her thrown away Cindy."

"Listen Sweetie," said Mom, "we're so sorry that our choice to love one another is causing you problems at school. These people are not really your friends if they hurt your feelings this way. Do you tell the teacher that they are teasing you?"

"Yes, she knows. She tells them to use kind words, and she tells me not to worry because some people don't understand. But, why can't you just be with my dad?"

"Well, Sarah, being with your dad is not an option. Your dad and I love you very much. That won't ever change. But Daddy and I don't love each other that way anymore. It has nothing to do with you though. You are loved and so are your friends, Jack and Cindy."

"You're right Mom. Linda is very kind to me. She treats me like you treat me. She goes to all my games and performances at school. Daddy hasn't been to every game, but Linda has."

Mom looked Sarah in her eyes. "Now wait a minute Sarah, that's not fair. Your dad works a lot and he does his best to try to support you. All of us love you, but Linda cannot and will not replace your dad."

"I know, Mom. I love you all. I understand. I'll try to explain to my friends why my family looks different and how loved I am.

Love is what matters most and I feel loved!

THE END

Other titles by this author:

Amazon.com   *TaneshaHopson.com*

If you like good reads in your classroom, or at home, there are several helpful resources available. Hopefully, this book helped you get the conversation started. To keep the conversation going, try some of these books.

Mommy's Family by: Nancy Garden.

Daddy, Papa and Me by: Leslea Newman.

And Tango Makes Three by: Justin Richardson and Peter Parnell

Peter Riley

HOLMFIRTH
A Bygone Era

P & D Riley

First published 2006
Reprinted 2007
Reprinted 2008

P & D Riley
12 Bridgeway East
Cheshire
WA7 6LD
England

ISBN: 1 874712 72 7

British Library Cataloguing in Publication Data
A catalogue record for this book is available from the British Library

Printed in England by JPS Design & Print

Introduction

The small Yorkshire town of Holmfirth has had a varied existence to say the least, with textiles, sheep, filming, saucy postcard production and TV all playing a major part in bringing it to public attention in the past 100 years.

Today, of course, Holmfirth is world famous as the home to the world's longest running comedy series *Last of the Summer Wine*, but there is more to the town and surrounding areas than the show, excellent though it is. Holmfirth is a haven for walking, hiking and cycling, with wildlife watching also playing its role.

The town has also had tragedy, with major floods hitting Holmfirth in 1777, 1852 and 1944 which killed many locals and changed the town forever.

What surprises many visitors today is that Holmfirth was considered the Hollywood of its days, with early, silent, feature films being made locally by the Bamforth family, who were years ahead of the California moguls, and many film buffs believe that Bamforth's were responsible for producing the world's first movie about the tragic loss of the luxury liner *Titanic* in 1912.

The wonderful thing about Holmfirth, and its surrounding villages, is that they have remained almost timeless. The solid stone buildings that make up most of the area remain as they have been for generations, with planners resisting the urge to tear down its history and replace it with something more modern and undoubtedly ugly; and certainly with something less enduring than the properties built by those genius Victorians!

This small book is not intended to be a comprehensive history of Holmfirth, rather it offers a small sample of the long saga of the town and its people which, I hope, will be welcomed by the many thousands who visit the town every year.

Peter Riley

Acknowledgements

Huddersfield Metropolitan Borough Council, Local History Library
Holmfirth Tourist Information Centre
Holmfirth Public Library
PDM Associates
On The Air Magazine
(www.ontheairmagazine.com)
Historical Investigations

By The Same Author

Haigh Hall and The Bradshaigh Family; The Highways and Byways of Sherlock Holmes;
The Highways and Byways of Jack the Ripper; Heaton Hall and the Egerton Family;
Wythenshawe Hall and the Tatton Family; Manchester Then and Now; Pits and Looms;
Warrington Then and Now; Leigh Then and Now; A Short History of Culcheth (with Oscar Plant);
Leigh, Tyldesley and Atherton A Bygone Era; Newton-le-Willows A Bygone Era;
The World of Crime (with Mark Llewellin); Wythenshawe A Bygone Era (with Susan Hall);
A History of Peel Hall; Bramall Hall and the Davenport family

One

FOR a thousand years the tiny hamlet of Holmfirth lay snuggled in the Holme Valley, a forgotten, timeless community of a few dozen souls earning their living by traditional Yorkshire trades such as sheep rearing, forestry and hill farming.

The first recorded settlers date back to the 10th century, though it is more than likely that there were people living in the area even before that, many in tiny clearings in the forest. Indeed in Saxon times the forest at Holmfirth was owned by the lords of Wakefield, with history telling us that the very name Holmfirth means *woodland belonging to Holme*; in other words a forested land belonging to the Holme valley.

A survey in the 14th century also tells us that there were only 175 inhabitants in Holmfirth, or at least families, since a married couple counted as one taxable unit! By the very nature of such a tiny population it is obvious that there was no room for any type of industry other than, perhaps, a blacksmith's shop for the shoeing of local horses and of those travelling the highways and byways of Holmfirth.

In 1476 the hamlet's first stone church was erected close to the river Holme, on the site of an earlier wooden one, and just a quarter of a century later a chapel-of-ease was also built in Holmfirth making it unnecessary for travellers or residents to travel to their nearest one at Almondbury Parish Church five miles away.

A chapel of ease was a church building apart from the main church of a parish and was usually much more accessible to many parishoners than the main parish church and normally existed when a parish covered many widely spread villages, particularly in hilly districts such as the Holme Valley.

In 1650 residents petitioned for Holmfirth to become a separate parish, having been an integral part of Almondbury parish until that time. This was granted a year later, though its independent status did not last long, for only a decade later it became once again a chapel of ease and there has been speculation among historians that the privilege of being a separate parish was taken from Holmfirth as punishment for its support of Oliver Cromwell and his Parliamentary army during the English Civil War.

This is a likely scenario for it is common knowledge that revenge played a part in the aftermath of the Civil War among supporters of Charles II, with even Cromwell's body being dug up and 'executed' as a warning to the country not to

---

HOLMFIRTH, a chapelry and town, partly in the parish of Almondbury, but chiefly in that of Kirkburton, Wapentake of Upper Agbrigg, West Riding county York, 6 miles S. of Huddersfield. It is a station on the Manchester, Sheffield, and Lincolnshire railway. It is a large manufacturing village, and polling place for the West Riding, situated in a vale watered by the river Holm, over which are two stone bridges, and sheltered by lofty hills. The town, which is of modern growth, is irregularly built, but is well paved and lighted. The inhabitants are principally engaged in the manufacture of woollen cloth, for which the numerous springs of clear soft water in the vicinity render it particularly well adapted. The machinery of the mills is impelled by the powerful streams which descend from the hills, and by water collected in three reservoirs formed at the cost of £30,000. Many of the inhabitants are also engaged in the extensive collieries, and some in business at Huddersfield. The living is a perpetual curacy in the diocese of Ripon, value £150, in the patronage of the Vicar of Kirkburton. There are places of worship for Wesleyans, Roman Catholics, and Baptists, and several schools. Fairs are held on the Saturday following 27th March, and 28th October, and before Old May Day.

Extract from The National Gazetteer of Great Britain and Ireland 1868

trifle with royalty again! That Holmfirth supported the Parliamentarians against the Royalists of Charles I is evident from records which show that the town sent 100 musketeers to fight on Cromwell's behalf, though it has never been made clear why the district decided to support Parliament rather than the king, though it could be that the Yorkshire leaders at the time thought it high handed of King Charles I to travel from London and set up his court in York, proclaiming it his *de facto* capital of England for the duration.

It was a decision that the king undoubtedly regretted, for a map shows the state of play between the opposing sides, with the royalists finding themselves hemmed in in this part of Yorkshire.

But Yorkshire played a major part in the Civil War and it was inevitable that some residents in Holmfirth would want to play their part too, and when Lord

A print showing musketeers off to fight in the Civil War

Fairfax, the leading parliamentarian commander in Yorkshire in 1642, called for volunteers to build an army in the region he succeeded in recruiting 900 men from around Yorkshire to help him occupy Tadcaster.

Although Fairfax was forced to flee after being outnumbered by the Earl of Newcastle's royalist army, the parliamentarians were eventually holed up in Bradford where it became a focal point for parliamentarian resistance in the West Riding of Yorkshire, and was reinforced by volunteers of the type of soldiers who took up arms in Holmfirth.

Right: How the opposing sides in the English Civil War lined up for battle

Two

IN the years after the Civil War Holmfirth and the entire Holme Valley returned to some sort of normality, with farming and cottage industries playing a major role. For most residents, living in the Holme Valley meant their cottages were perched atop the many hillsides that are such an attractive feature of the area, for there was no real reason for them to live in the valley proper, as this would have meant unnecessary toil when moving from one part of the district to another; and with hill farming being the dominent employment for so many years, it made sense to live nearer the work.

However, change was on the way, whether Holmfirth villagers liked it or not, and by the 18th century a woollen clothier named John Fallas was to be the catalyst that would change the way of life forever. Fallas bought land and property in the bottom of the valley and he was responsible for bringing the Industrial Revolution to this part of West Yorkshire.

He soon ordered mills to be built, cottages to be erected, and a workforce brought in to keep the mills running, all of which was possible only because of the proximity of the mills to the Holme and Ribble rivers. At the start of the industrialisation of this part of the valley, Holmfirth had grown considerably and its population outranked that of Leeds and nearby Huddersfield, so there was a willing and able workforce to help build the empire that was eventually to ensure that Britain was world leader in textiles.

The growth of the cotton industry saw the introduction of the revolutionary Spinning Jenny into Holmfirth in 1776, and while our American cousins were starting a revolution in North America in that same year, so too in Yorkshire was discontent brewing, and it soon became obvious that while many people were employed in the mills, the growth of the new technology also brought an underbelly of poverty, with many families who had always survived by their cottage industries and hand looms, now finding themselves unable to compete with the massive machines.

The result of the discontent in the town saw the emergence of the Luddite movement who were determined to wreck the new-fangled machinery and close the mills, thus returning to the status-quo. Violence broke out in Holmfirth but, of course, it was not going to make any difference to progress and the Luddite movement gradually ceased to exist and the mills of Holmfirth went on the gain a well deserved reputation for producing some of the finest cloth in the British Empire.

As the 19th century dawned the growth of industrialism in Britain grew at a rapid pace, and with it the mills of Holmfirth, and it was timely that in the 1830s a new invention came on the scene - railways - and it was to make a major change in the way goods were shipped.

Holmfirth railway station opened for business in 1850, as a branch of the Lancashire and Yorkshire Railway Company, and mill owners were quick to start sending horse drawn lorries and carts to Station Road with their goods which could then be sent quickly and cheaply to ports around the country and thus to Britain's colonies and dominions.

The railway station was also hugely popular with the residents of Holmfirth for it gave them the opportunity to leave the town and see other parts of Yorkshire, or any part of England, for the first time in their lives, and it is recorded that only a year after the station opened for business 1,190 passengers left Holmfirth for nearby Huddersfield where a festival in Honley was being held.

In 1852 more than 3,000 passengers travelled from Holmfirth station for a

Sunday evening trip to Penistone, a small market town situated about half way between Huddersfield and Sheffield.

As the Holme Valley, and Holmfirth in particular, continued to boom, it soon became necessary to look at other ways of improving the lot of those who lived and worked there, and in 1837 an Act of Parliament gave the go-ahead for the construction of a number of reservoirs. That decision was to influence the wealth of the region and shape the way local people lived their lives. But it also had a disastrous side, for in 1852 the people of Holmfirth suffered its worst ever disaster when, on February 5, at the height of the winter rains, the Bilberry Reservoir at Holme Village burst its banks and caused a massive flood.

Floodwater swept down the valley and into Holmfirth, claiming 81 lives and thou-

Sheep shearing at Holmfirth in 1900. This was still an important industry in the town.

sands of pounds worth of damage. There had been a flood in 1777 but that was nothing compared to the major sweep of water that took Holmfirth in its grip in the 1852 torrent.

The flood followed heavy rain and it was reported that construction defects in the reservoir were largely responsible for the tragedy which was widely reported in the national newspapers of the day.

One newspaper later reported: "This calamity attracted at the time the attention of the whole nation, and aroused the benevolent sympathy of all classes, from the Queen on the throne to the humblest persons in the realm who had a heart to feel for the sufferings of their fellow men."

So severe was the flood that stones weighing as much as four tons were swept down the valley and stacks of debris reaching to the second floor of local factories was reported. Queen Victoria and Prince Albert sent a message of sympathy to

Holmfirth from Victoria Bridge after the devastating flood of 1852

View from Mill Hill looking towards Victoria Bridge showing flood damage

Holmfirth and emergency fund raising was started to help those who had lost everything.

In Holmfirth town centre Victoria Bridge was demolished by the sheer weight and power of the water, with many local shops being flooded and severely damaged. Remarkably the town's parish church was let off lightly and sustained no severe damage, though one of the churchyard's huge pillars was wrenched from its foundations and flung aside.

The Wesleyan chapel in the town was flooded to about three feet in depth, and the graveyard surrounding the chapel was severely damaged, though, luckily, the homes the the minsters were built on higher grounds and thus were saved from the worst of the floodwater, and their families were able to get out in time and shelter higher up the hillside.

There were reports of coffins being washed up and swept away and, ironically, one of the coffins that was broken open by the strength of the water and swept away with the corpse was that of local businessman John Harpin, who had been one of the main promoters of the scheme to build strong reservoirs in the Holme Valley.

Remains of Upper Bridge, 1852

At the time of the 1852 flood Holmfirth had a population of about six thousand, so it was a devastating blow for the whole town since it affected so many families either directly or indirectly, with local businesses and shops being swept out of existence; but it was the terrible number of people killed that touched the heart of the nation, particularly since so many died in their beds after the flood swept through the town at one-o-clock in the morning.

On February 14, 1852, the prestigious *London Illustrated News* published a long report on the disaster, and the following extract serves to show how the rest of Britain would receive the news over a week later:

"On Thursday morning, the 5th instant, at one-o-clock, the inhabitants of Holmfirth were suddenly overwhelmed by a mountainous mass of water which, bursting through an extensive reservoir, hurried them without a moment's warning into eternity.

"A more complete wreck, a more melancholy scene than Holmfirth presented to the thousands who visited it on Thursday, has never been beheld. The streets were filled with broken furniture, carding machines, huge iron boilers, bags of wool and other things; and the graveyards had their dead dislodged, and their contents borne again to the doors of the living.

"The 'Holme reservoirs' are three in number, and are formed at the top of the hills some distance from each other. They are called 'the Bilberry,' 'the Holmestyes' and 'the Bawshaw' reservoirs. They were made under the authority of an Act of Parliament passed in 1840.

The particular reservoir which has caused the present destruction if 'the Bilberry'.

"The embankment of the reservoir has always been, from being leaky, been regarded as unsafe, and from time to time rumours have been circulated in Holmfirth that it was likely to give way. Some of the company's servants, it is said, were watching it on the Wednesday before the accident and, in consequence of what transpired, the whole of the families connected near the reservoir, fortunately removed the night before. Had they not done so, there would doubtless have been a serious addition to the present fearful loss of life.

"The rumours which induced the parties at Digley to remove were current in Holmfirth the same evening; but, unfortunately, the inhabitants disregarded them and retired to bed, hoping that all would be well.

"It appears the pent-up waters burst their barrier a little after one-on-clock on Thursday morning, and in a resistless and mighty torrent swept away all obstacles..."

Over 60 bodies were collected for possible identification and interment at different periods in the days following the disaster, many in the villages on the adjoining hills or up in the valley but even internment presented a major problem, for when seven bodies were taken to be buried at Holmebridge Church the graves were full of water and the churchyard had suffered such severe damage that their burials were delayed and bodies were placed inside the church itself until damage clearance allowed the internments to be be carried out properly.

An inquest, which lasted five days, was held into the deaths of the victims of the disaster and the jury of fifteen concluded: "We find that the deceased persons came to their deaths by drowning, caused by the bursting of the Bilberry Reservoir."

The verdict was also damning against those it concluded were responsible, and went on: "We also find that the Bilberry Reservoir was defective in its original construction, and that the commissioners, the engineer, and the overlooker were greatly culpable in not seeing to the proper regulation of the works; and we also

The bodies of those who died in the Great Flood of 1852 were collected in groups and taken to various public houses in and around Holmfirth

New Inn: Hinchcliffe Mill - James Booth, 60; Nancy Booth, 44; Lydia and Hannah Brook; Elizabeth Dodd, 7; Sarah Hannah Dodd, 17 months; Martha Hinchcliffe, a child; Nancy Marsden, 53; Charles Crosland.

George Inn: Holmfirth - Jonathon Crosland, 39; Joshua Crosland, 21; Mary Hellawell, 28; George Hellawell, 9; Sarah Hellawell, 6; Elizabeth Hellawell, 4; John Hellawell, 2; Ann Hellawell, 10 months; Hannah Dodd, 30.

Elephant and Castle, Holmfirth - James Lee, 65; Joe Marsden, 18; William Exley, 31; Eliza Matthews (of Shepley and a servant to the Greenwood family at Tollgate), 12; Lydia Greenwood, 45.

White Hart, Holmfirth - Hannah Crosland, 17; Ellen Wood, 22; James Charlesworth, 14; Alfred Woodcock, 17; Emily Sandford; and an unidentified female.

Shoulder of Mutton, Holmfirth - Amelia Fearns, 23; Joshual Charlesworth, 16; an unidentified boy aged about 11.

Rose and Crown, Holmfirth - Eliza Marsden, 46.

Kings Head - Abel Earnshaw, aged 6.

Waggon and Horses - Joe Mettrick, aged 1; unidentified female about 4 years old.

Crown Hotel - Sydney Hartley; George Hartley, 10 weeks; Charles Earnshaw, 36; John Ashall, 32; his wife (no name given) 30; Sarah Jane Sandford, 9; Martha Crosland, 15.

Rose and Crown, Thongsbridge - Hannah Bailey, 30; an infant (possibly Hannah Bailey's); Hannah Shackleton, 8.

Royal Oak, Thongsbridge - Joshua Earnshaw, 72; Tamor Shackleton, 33, James Shackleton, aged 1 (son of Tamor Shackleton); Elizabeth Hartley, 4; unidentied girl aged about 4.

Rock Inn, Smithy Place - William Mettrick, 31; daughter of Matthew Fearns (name unknown), 6 months.

Travellers Inn, Honley - Mary Anne Hartley, 39; James Hartley, 14; Alfred Mettrick, 8; unidentified boy about 4.

Jacob's Well, Honley - Martha Hartley, 39; Charles Thorpe, 3; Betty Healey, 7; unidentified boy about 6.

Golden Fleece, Armitage Bridge - Girl identified as daughter of Aner Bailey; unidentified boy (records state that the girl was first stated to be named Mettrick but was later claimed to be called Hartley. At the inquest, however, Aner Bailey said it was his child and he was allowed to inter her.)

Oddfellow's Arms, Big Valley - Rose Charlesworth, 39.

A view of Holmfirth town centre in the mid-20th century when traffic was almost non-existent compared with the heavy flow that snakes through the town today, showing clearly how the town was built in the bottom of the Holme Valley, close to the river.

find that the commissioners, in permitting the Bilberry reservoir to remain for several years in a dangerous state, with a full knowledge thereof, and not lowering the waste pit, have been guilty of great and culpable negligence; and we regret that, the reservoir being under the management of a corporation, prevent us bringing in a verdict of manslaughter, as we are convinced that the gross and culpable negligence of the commissioners would have sub-

HEIGHT OF THE FLOOD CAUSED BY THE BURSTING OF BILBERRY RESERVOIR. FEB. 5TH 1852.

Memorial stone in Holmfirth town centre to the 1852 flood

jected them to such a verdict had they been in the position of an individual or firm."

The Government Inspector placed in charge of finding out what caused the disaster was a Captain Moody, and he reported his findings in his report which concluded: "In this neighbourhood there are many mountain reservoirs receiving floods of water, impounded by lofty dams; pray don't look upon them and treat them like mill-dams or fish ponds. They are engines of mighty force, strong in aid of your industry to augment your wealth, and terrible in their power to destroy if mismanaged or neglected.

"The fact must be indelibly impressed on the minds of all the dwellers in Holmfirth."

A disaster fund was set up for the relief of the town's destitute and bereaved, with cash donations being sent to Holmfirth from across the country, and in total more than £69,000 was raised, a huge sum for those days, and this figure shows the deep impact the Holmfirth flood had on the hearts and minds of the British people.

Three

IN the years following the 1852 flood Holmfirth slowly recovered, and by the 1870s a new industry sprung up in the town - one that could have brought it massive-fame and fortune if the weather in this part of the world had been kinder. That industry was photography, and one man in Holmfirth was quick to realise the potential of this new-fangled invention; he was James Bamforth who quickly became a keen photographer. Already an accomplished artist Bamforth decided that the two could go together and he spent months developing silent films and producing the artwork for picture postcards.

While Holmfirth never quite made it as Yorkshire's answer to Hollywood, it certainly made a major impact on the British holiday scene. James Bamforth spent weeks painting lifesize backdrops to his silent movies and also produced over 600 Magic Lantern slides each year. In postcard production the Bamforth family were head and shoulders above any possible rival and they centred their attention at the end of the 19th century and the beginning of the 20th on romantic pictures and sentimental scenes, all of which catered for a growing market, particularly when millions of men throughout Britain were sent off the fight in the First World War when sentimental messages were almost a way of life.

However, after the war the British working class were also realising that they could now afford to spend at least some of their time having a well-deserved holi-

Right::
The former Bamforth's famous postcard factory in Holmfirth pictured in 2006

Below:
Just one of the millions of picture postcards produced by Bamforth's which were sold in seaside resorts.

day by the seaside, and here, too, the Bamforth family hit the big time with their idea for producing 'saucy' picture postcards to be sent home to family and friends.

The First World War put paid to Holmfirth's ambitions to be a major movie producing town and they ceased film production.

Producing picture postcards, particularly those with *double entendres*, sold by the million, and at its height the firm are reported to have produced as many as sixteen million in one year! Production of the postcards ceased in Holmfirth in the early 1990s and the assets of Bamforth's were bought by a Leeds based company. Bamforth's may have gone but their old factory can still be seen in the centre of the town, though there is plans for redevelopment of the site.

Just across the river from the factory stands the Holmfirth Picturedrome, which was built in 1912 and opened to the public on March 1, 1913, - Easter Monday. It has played a major part in providing entertainment for the people of Holmfirth since that time, and was a huge undertaking for such a compact town, with 1,040 seats.

Strangely the projection box for showing all those intriguing old films was outside the main building and electricity for lighting was produced from a gas generator stored in an outbuilding! It is also believed that the projectors were generated by hand.

Originally known as the Holme Valley Theatre, the theatre also had live performances with a music hall flavour, including singers, musicians and even a strong man act. But it was cinema that was the popular form of entertainment from the 1920s onwards, and in 1930 the first sound movie in the theatre was *Sunnyside Up*, which proved hugely popular, or at least fascinating to an audience who had never seen such sophistication before!

The Picturedrome continued as a cinema until 1967 when dwindling audiences meant the inevitable end to this type of entertainment in the town, and, like thousands of other former cinemas in Britain, it was converted into a bingo hall until even this type of amusement was overshadowed by the emergence of more varied forms of entertainment, particularly satellite television, and in the early 1990s it shut its doors and remained empty for the next four years.

In 1997 it was purchased by a local businessman and renovated so a standards suitable for a variety of uses, including its ground floor being converted for use as a cinema which was also capable of staging live performances, thus giving voice to the old maxim: "What goes around, comes around!"

The Picturedrome in Holmfirth

View across the river to the Parish Church from outisde the Picturedrome

Four

DURING the middle of the 10th century the growth of Holmfirth seemed assured, with industry and farming working side by side, though today it is difficult for visitors to picture the days when more than 60 mills pumped steam and smoke into the town and its surrounding countryside.

Mills certainly played their part in providing work for thousands of people throughout the Holme Valley, and more than 20 mills were in production thanks to the River Holme and its tributaries between Holmfirth and Holme village.

But on Whit Monday, 1944, while British forces were preparing to invade Europe with their allies, another, more present danger, was facing the people of Holmfirth with yet another flood. Nicknamed the 'forgotten flood' because it didn't even make the pages of the nation's newspapers because of a news blackout prior to the Normandy invasion.

Though nothing like as devastating or lethal as the 1852 flood the flood nevertheless caused heartache to the residents of Holmfirth. Spring rain in the Holme Valley had caused the River Holme to flood and rushing water caused buildings and foundation supports to collapse in the centre of the town.

Many of the buildings were constructed upon supporting piles but the power of the flood washed these away, and big holes were left in roads and empty spaces were left in Victorian Street and Hollowgate where shops had once stood. Many houses which remained were flooded and neighbours found themselves acting as good samaritans to those who had been unfortunate enough to have their homes destroyed.

There was an emergency feeding station set up in Holmfirth Wesleyan Chapel and the power of the flood was only realised afterwards when scars were left on the town and mud banks showed the height of flood water. It reached to the top of living rooms in many places, including properties in Scar Fold, and invaded a tunnel underneath the historic Elephant and Castle public house, where a brass plate showing the height of the floodwater can be seen to this day.

It took a long time for everything to get back into shape in Holmfirth after the flood, and many residents wondered how long it would be before another disaster would hit the town? What is surprising is that the town survived yet another major

Devastation is clearly shown in this picture of flooding in Holmfirth in 1944

Hollowgate, Holmfirth, pictured in 1944, showing flood damage

catastrophe to get back on its feet even in the midst of wartime. But survive Holmfirth certainly did and with the building of the Digley Reservoir in 1954 the town breathed a sigh of relief, for it meant, theoretically at least, that no such similar disaster could strike Holmfirth again.

Holmfirth visitors who call into Daisy Lane Books in Towngate will be surprised to learn that this 250 years old building was once the town Constable's house and lockup. The building dates back to 1597 and was once used for collecting taxes, with those who failed to pay up facing a period in the tiny jail.

Five

IN 1971 Holmfirth first said welcome to the BBC as it sent a small TV unit into the town to start filming an episode of its popular *Comedy Playhouse* series. The town was chosen to backdrop the programme which was given the rather unassuming title of *The Last of the Summer Wine*. It was fully expected that the show would be a one-off as it was intended to highlight the talent of unknown writer Roy Clarke. It was an assumption that proved to be profoundly wrong, for such was the humour, the tremendous cast and the strong writing of Roy Clarke, that the BBC were soon overwhelmed with viewers' reactions.

It didn't take long for the BBC mandarins in London to realise that here was something different in the comedy stakes. Here was a show primarily about three retired men who had plenty of time on their hands and were trying to act like the schoolboy chums they once were. It was an unusual format, but one that held immediate appeal with viewers, and with a strangely haunting theme tune from composer Ronnie Hazlehurst the BBC had a hit on their hands.

Of course it was the choice of cast that made such a major impact, especially in the scruffy character of 'Compo', played by veteran actor Bill Owen, Norman Clegg, played ever since by Peter Sallis, Blamire, the know-it-all, played by Michael Bates, and wrinkled stocking queen nosy neighbour Nora Batty, played continually by veteran actress Kathy Staff.

In those days Holmfirth was completely unknown outside Yorkshire, except perhaps by collectors of Bamforth's saucy postcards, but with *Last of the Summer Wine*(the word 'The' was later dropped from the title) taking to the airwaves that was soon to change, and Holmfirth became a tourist mecca.

Sid's Cafe opposite the parish church. Now a 'must' see place for Summer Wine enthusiasts in Holmfirth

Nora Batty's famous front door and steps just off Huddersfield Road

Today thousands of people from across the world visit Holmfirth to walk the tiny streets where the characters walk, hoping to catch a glimpse of them filming. The series has given Holmfirth a new lease of life to its many small businesses, many of whom thrive off the popularity of the series.

The cottage which is home to Nora Batty is now a recognised tourist spot and has even been given its own three star catering award by Yorkshire tourist chiefs, and it is even possible to rent out the house for holidays in the town.

Sid's Cafe, opposite the parish church, is another 'must see' stopping off place for visitors as this setting has been used for more than 30 years and it has often featured as a 'drop in' place for Compo, Clegg and friends who faced up to the forocity of 'Ivy', (played by Jane Freeman) who served tea and cakes to the old scallawags in a most impolite manner!

The almost deserted streets of Holmfirth before *Last of the Summer Wine* brought tourists flooding in

The history of Holmfirth is a long one, with many changes being faced by its citizens with strength and fortitude. It may not have achieved its rank as the film capital of the world; it may have been devastated with floods and war, but the fact is that for more than three decades Holmfirth has welcomed visitors from around the world, (many intruding in private homes, in the hope of catching a glimpse of the TV stars that have made the town so famous) with patience and good humour, and that is something money cannot buy!

Cast and crew of *Last of the Summer Wine* discuss their next moves during a filming session

Left: The former constable's house and lockup as it looks today

Top right: Towngate and South Lane in the 1960s

Bottom Right: Holmfirth parish church

An atmospheric photograph of Towngate, believed to be in the 1940s